# ALL IT TAKES TO BE A GOOD MOTHER

Ayesha G. Bailey

All it takes to be a good mother

All right reserved . No part of this publication may be reproduced, distributed, or transmitted in any form or by any means including photocopying recording, or other electronic or mechanical methods, without the prior written permission of the publisher, except in the case of brief quotations embodied in critical reviews and certain other non-commercial uses permitted copyright law

Copyright@Ayesha G. Bailey,2022

All it takes to be a good mother

Table of content

# CHAPTER ONE: What Motherhood is!

Motherhood is the state of being a mama. A person enters fatherhood when they come to a mama. This most generally happens when their child is born, but it can also be through relinquishment or by marrying or getting a mate to someone with children. Motherhood is a gender-specific interpretation of the term parenting.

masters are one of the first suggestions of the sovereignty of God in our lives. masters educate us to have confidence and belief in ourselves. masters knew from experience how important it is for people to believe in themselves in order for children to be whole, strong, and grow with a healthy estimation of themselves.

masters play a critical part in the family, which is an important force for social cohesion and integration. The mama-child relationship is vital for the healthy development of children. And matters

aren't only caregivers; they're also breadwinners for their families. Yet women continue to face major -- and indeed life- changing -- challenges in fatherhood.

Parturition, which should be a cause for festivity, is a grave health threat for too numerous women in developing countries. perfecting motherly health is the Millennium Development thing on which the least progress has been made. A woman in a least-developed country is 300 times more likely to die in parturition or from gestation-related complications than a woman in an advanced country. We must make gestation and parturition safer by enabling health systems to give family planning, professed attendance at birth, and exigency obstetric care.

Violence against women, numerous of whom are maters

, remains one of the most pervasive mortal rights violations of our time. It has far-reaching consequences -- venturing the lives of women and girls, harming their families and communities, and damaging the veritable fabric of societies. Ending and precluding violence against women should be a crucial precedence for all countries.

We must also ensure universal access to education. The benefits of educating women and girls accrue not only to individual families but to whole countries, unleashing the eventuality of women to contribute to broader development. Statistics also show that educated maters

All it takes to be a good mother

are much more likely to keep their children in the academy, meaning that the benefits of education transcend generations.

As we strive to support matters

In their caregiving work, we should develop and expand family-friendly programs and services, similar to childcare centers, that would reduce some of the workload placed on women. Women and men likewise need stronger public support to partake inversely in work and family liabilities. Families erected on the recognition of equivalency between women and men will contribute to more stable and productive societies.

# CHAPTER TWO: How a Good Wife treats Her Husband

How does a man want to be treated?
How do you treat your man in a relationship?
What are some effects a woman should have on her man?
How a woman should treat a man – 20 ways to do it right
Takeaway

Men earn as important and excellent treatment as women. After all, they've been putting trouble into a relationship for a long time. All of the points mentioned above highlight how to treat a man in a relationship.
How should a woman treat a man? In our society, there has been so much important advice and exchanges on how to treat a woman right. Still, little has been bandied about how women should treat men.

Why is it that way? Does it mean men don't deserve to be treated right, or their passions aren't valued? There are effects a woman should do for a man to make him feel appreciated.

Men also want to be cocked and watched for like their mates. Sadly, some women are so focused on themselves that they occasionally forget their men's feelings and requirements.

utmost men need someone that authentically understands how to treat a man. especially, a woman should treat her man as well as she'd have anticipated from him. When a man sees the trouble you put into making him happy, he's empowered to do further for you.

How should a woman treat a man also? Are there effects a woman should have on her man? Read this composition to the end to learn how women should treat men.

Most men want women who know how to treat a man right. Thankfully, how to treat a man in a relationship doesn't bear special chops or assignments.

As a woman, you have presumably been treated right numerous times in your life. To treat your man right, all you need is to repay. This time around, you'll be more purposeful in making your man happy.

Specifically, men like to be treated like babies( not literally), but men also crave the 100% attention, care, and coddling the kiddies get. He wants you to show genuine respect for his well-being. He wants you to be kind and compassionate.

Unlike what some people believe, men are also emotional. So, it would help if you watched about their passions when you talk or act. Show that you watch when he's emotionally worried and be there for him.

All it takes to be a good mother

In fact, most men don't want you to buy precious effects or give them to a plutocrat. Being kind, loving, minding, and compassionate is enough for anyone. You have the key to his heart if you can treat your man right or you know how to treat a man right.
Women who are designedly minding about their men want to know how to treat a man in a relationship.

Luckily for you, treating a man isn't rocket wisdom. It's a commodity you can learn. It'll make your man feel good and strengthen your relationship.
As a woman, you have to treat a man like he's the only bone
you have ever loved. Indeed, you might have been in other connections in history, but your present man must feel good anytime he's with you.

A real woman treats her man like he's stylish. Let him feel safe and defended around you. No matter what he may have faced outdoors, your presence should lighten his mood and ameliorate him.
Your man wants to know you have his reverse at all times. He shouldn't have to supplicate for your attention; it should come snappily.

youthful couple relaxing together

What are some effects a woman should do for her man?

Again, men don't ask for importance in how they should be treated. They want the same thing as women, but there are specific effects a woman should do for her man.

1. Buy him gifts

One thing a woman should do for her man is to get him gifts. As much as you love bouquets, your man also appreciates it with other precious particulars.

Don't suppose he won't value it because the gift doesn't equal the bones

he has given you in the history. What matters is the gesture.

2. Call and return his calls

Whether your man calls frequently or not, you should make communication part of your routine. Please don't stay until he calls or textbooks. Call him at arbitrary and at will. These calls will assure him of your love, commitment, and fidelity.

3. Praise him

You should be your man's cheerleader. He knows he's trying his best, but he should hear it from you. Remind him of his stylish rates and how you wouldn't trade them for anything.

4. Help him with ménage chores

Although numerous women are formerly doing this, it's worth mentioning. Your man will appreciate it if you help him with house chores. It doesn't reduce your worth; it means you know when to help out.

5. Know what's important to him

A woman treats her man right by knowing what's important to him. Flash back, men don't speak their minds like women. Still, you'll notice effects precious to him through how he talks or treats people or effects.

Woman hugging her hubby from behind

How a woman should treat a man – 20 ways to do it right

Someone that truly understands how to treat a man will always have her way with men. The tips below will show you how women should treat men or how to treat a man like a king.

1. Treat him with love and watch

Saying is easier than doing. You have presumably told your man you love him, but he needs to see you in action. Everything you do around him should be to assure him of your love.

Be loving, caring, faithful, and kind to him. Don't ever give him reasons to misdoubt your love.

How should a woman treat a man? Start by harkening to him when he talks. Men appreciate women who are active listeners. It gives them peace of mind knowing they can tell their mates anything in the world without being judged or blamed.

All it takes to be a good mother

4. Treat him like a baby

Do you want to know how to treat a man, also try imagining your man as a baby. Babies can't talk, but you need to give them full attention and care.

In the case of a man, it looks like you're taking care of an overgrown man. But occasionally, men want to feel putrefied too. They've always been tutored to take care of their women and that any little care you show will admit enormous appreciation.

Treat your man like a king by taking him to a fancy eatery or an instigative place. ensure it comes as a surprise by informing him out of the blue.

For illustration, tell him to get ready on Saturday that you both will be visiting a place together. This will make him agitated and look forward to the day.

Learn about stupendous date ideas in this videotape

6. Let him be vulnerable

Men aren't known to be emotionally suggestive as women. Still, they can be the most vulnerable when they feel safe around you. When he shows his weakness in front of you, embrace him and let him know everything will be fine.

All it takes to be a good mother

Don't ever use this against him.

7. Be vulnerable

still, you should repay, If your man feels safe emotionally around you. Don't regard others as your confidante while you leave your man hanging. Learn to open up to him whenever you're down.

Seek his advice and let him know how important his followership meant to you. This makes him feel like your protection.

Do you want to know how to treat your swain? blarney his idol instinct. According to James Bauer, the idol instinct proposition states that men like to be Superman around the people they love.

Your task is to ask your man to help you whenever demanded. He wants you to be impressed and fulfilled. That means they want to be there for their loved bones in all ramifications.

9. Don't compare him to other men

Nothing breaks a man's heart than comparison with other men. It's the height of sport and discourteousness to him. But you shouldn't rub it in your man's face. Men aren't equal in their responsibility to their loved bones

.

Don’t be that gal that raises eyebrows when you see him having fun with his musketeers.

11. respects him frequently

How do you treat your man? Shower him with great respects. Congratulate his dressing, shoes, haircuts, and so on. Don’t just congratulate him when he buys a new commodity, but also on other days when he least anticipated it. That makes him feel asked.

12. Be tender

How to treat a man, right? Be more romantic. Make every moment count with your mate. Hug him and kiss him when he returns from work or anywhere. When you're outdoors, reach out to hold his hands.

These little gestures support the love between you and your mate and strengthen the relationship.

13. Be robotic

Treat your man right by being veritably robotic and purposeful about your love. Write him an appreciation letter and niche it into his fund moment. Take a perambulation around your neighborhood or an instigative place during the weekend.

Naturalness makes your mate look forward to spending time with you.

All it takes to be a good mother

enjoying fun and games in demesne

14. Flashback his requests

Don't forget that utmost men aren't as suggestive as utmost women. He might not repeat his words after telling you to do a commodity, or he may ask for a commodity.

Try as important as possible to flashback his requests, indeed the bones

he mentioned casually. This shows him that you always hear him.

15. Don't make him supplicate for your attention

No bone

should have to supplicate for another's attention.However, the feeling isn't collective, and you'll be wasting your time being in that relationship, If you have to. Your man deserves his stylish, and you should always try to be available whenever he seeks your presence.

still, let him know ahead of time without sounding discourteous, If you can't.

16. Understand him

Men like it when they don't have to explain much before the woman gets them. He'll vapor to his musketeers about how understanding you can be. For case, when he comes back late, don't make hypotheticals.

rather, tell him you know the commodity must have delayed him, and also ask the reason.

Your man needs your help in his business or job and other conditioning. For illustration, if he has a conflict with another person, your first instinct shouldn't be to judge the case.

rather, you should be probative. Indeed if he's at fault, you must be polite in presenting your opinion.

18. Be kind

When it seems like love can't hold mates together, kindness helps. A kind mate will be there for you no matter the hurdles you face. Show your man this kindness by being compassionate under grueling matters.

still, be patient and understanding, If your man makes a mistake.

Don't judge him. rather, clinch him and gentle him. Let him know people make miscalculations, and you're there for him.

How to treat a man like a king? Stay pious to him. Fidelity is a factual test of love in any relationship.However, you should not entertain other individualities, If you love your partner. Unless your man isn't faithful to you, you might not have any reason to cheat or flirt with another man.

20. Trust him

Trust helps to make a stable and healthy relationship. Women who authentically understand how to treat a man trust their man wholeheartedly.However, you must give him the same treatment, If you want your man to trust you.

Don't fear when you see him with other women. She could be a workmate or friend. Allow him to have his time, and you can joke about it later.

When he doesn't pick up your call incontinently, understand he might be busy or forget. But now assume he's doing commodity shady things.

Takeaway

Men earn as important excellent treatment as women. After all, they've been putting trouble into a relationship for a long time. All of the points mentioned above highlight how to treat a man in a relationship.

Flash back, it's the trouble you put in a relationship you'll get in return. Every relationship demands some work, and knowing how to treat a man right will make you a better mate.

# CHAPTER THREE: How to Raise a Responsible Son

Raising a thoughtful, well- rounded son can be a challenge. Some boys are slow to pick up social graces, more interested in videotape games or Pokémon than people. Some are roisterous to the point where they've a hard time fastening.

No matter what your son is like, we've 10 effective ways to nudge him toward becoming a happy, well- rounded person.

1. Give him some responsibility.

Following directions and finishing tasks are chops that are frequently slow to develop in boys. Practice helps. Ask your preschooler to bring you a ladle so you can stir the hotcake batter. Assign your grade- schooler a regular task to help take care of a pet.

A sense of responsibility will serve him well in academia – and your home life will run further easily, too.

2. Let him show his feelings.

Indeed in these enlightened times, boys are frequently anticipated to stifle their gashes and swallow their wrathfulness while girls are allowed more free rein with their feelings. When your son gets worried, let him express himself, as long as he is not being destructive or fully out of control.

Also, once he has regained control of his feelings, you can talk to him about what he is feeling and why. Help him label his passions, whether it's hurt or sad or angry.

3. Give him plenty of physical affection.

Studies have observed that mothers and daddies have lower physical contact with boys than with girls, a trend that starts in toddlerhood. But girls are not the only bones

who need to be held and snuggled. Leverages from Mom and Dad will help your son feel safe and secure.

As boys get aged, they are likely to wince down from leverages and kisses from parents, especially when musketeers are around. But indeed if they say they do not want it, they still need affection just as important. So you may need to give your son touches and hugs in ways that are a bit more sneaky – a quick clinch when no bone

is around, a girl on the reverse while working together in the kitchen.

4. Do not try to shut down his high- fire machine.

Boys tend to have a lot of energy, which can get pent-up if they do not have enough chances to run, climb, and blow off brumes. Just be sure to remind your son that there are times and places – the classroom, for illustration – where he will need to shift to a lower gear.

5. Do not worry if he is not acting" mannish" enough.

Indeed tough- joe fathers have a nurturing side. ( The good bones

, at least.) A little boy who likes to snuggle his stuffed creatures is developing chops that will serve him well in majority.

6. Give him chances to polish his social chops.

Most boys don't form close intimate gemütlichkeit as fluently as girls. They are more likely to play in groups and jockey for leadership. Help your son strengthen one- on- one gemütlichkeit by arranging playdates for him, and encouraging him to partake his toys, use his good mores, and generally play nice.

7. Make music part of his life.

rehearsing an instrument can give your son a precious sense of accomplishment. Studies suggest that music assignments can also edge a youthful child's thinking chops and ameliorate his memory.

Still, a children's chorus can be a fun musical exertion, If group conditioning is more your boy's thing. Another advantage Choruses exercise together, so you will not have to apply practice time at home too frequently. Taking him to musicals or musical theater is another option, if he is willing.

8. Encourage his interests, indeed if they are not" boy" conditioning.

Still, his musketeers may tease him, which can be hard to deal with, If your son wants to take cotillion assignments. But if you inseminate a strong sense of tone in your son and encourage him to accept other people's differences, it will be easier for him to deal with any teasing that comes from being" different."

So, if he wants to take cotillion assignments, let him. either, the coming time he may veritably well want to play baseball rather.

9. Get involved at the academy.

Talk with your son's school teacher regularly to find out his classroom strengths and sins. Let her know, too, what you suppose his strengths are. Cover his schoolwork( without doing the work yourself), and encourage him to read or at least hear a story at least once a day.

10. Praise the positive.

" Boy" geste

, indeed when it's age-applicable, it can be hard for grown-ups to deal with – and boys get plenty of correcting, reprimanding, and scolding in the academy and at home as a result. Parents of girls frequently complain that boys get all the attention in the classroom, but( at least at early periods), the importance of that attention is negative.

What can you do? Whenever possible, try to catch your son" being good." Let him know that you appreciate his sweats to gain tone- control and channel his energy into conditioning that is formative and satisfying.

# CHAPTER FOUR: Raise a Good Daughter

How do you raise an important girl and what does that mean?

important girls grow up feeling secure in themselves. They learn to take action, making positive choices about their own lives and doing positive effects for others. They suppose critically about the world around them. They express their passions and admit the passions and studies of others in caring ways. important girls feel good about themselves and grow up with a "can-do" station. Of course, strong girls may( like all of us) have times of instability and tone- distrustfulness, but these passions aren't paralyzing because the girls have learned to work through their problems. important girls will grow up to lead full, precious lives.

Here are some of our experts ' ideas to help you raise important daughters.

Encourage your son to pursue a passion. " Full engagement with an exertion she loves will give her the occasion to master challenges, which will boost her tone- regard and adaptability and affirm natural values rather than appearance. " Having a passion lets her go shoot baskets or play an instrument, for illustration, rather than being swept up in online drama. "

Let her have a voice in making opinions. “ Whenever possible, let her make formative choices about her life. Let her choose her own clothes, within applicable limits. Give her a voice in what after- academy conditioning she participates in and how numerous she wants to do( as long as it works for the rest of the family, too). Flashback that knowing what she cares about utmost will come from trying some effects and changing she doesn’t like them, as well as from changing effects she loves to do, ”. “ Your son might need to make a commitment for a short time for an exertion( one soccer season) but when that’s over, it’s okay to try something different! ”

Encourage her to break issues on her own rather than fixing effects for her. “ When parents take over, girls don’t develop the managing chops they need to handle situations on their own. Ask your son to consider three strategies she might use to deal with a situation, and also ask her about the possible issues. Let her decide what she wants to do( within reason). Indeed if you differ with her choice, you give your son a sense of control over her life and show her that she's responsible for her opinions

Encourage her to take physical pitfalls. “ Girls who avoid pitfalls have poorer tone- regard than girls who can and do face challenges, " `` appetite your son to go beyond her comfort zone — for illustration, encourage a girl who's spooked to ride her bike upward to find just a small hill to conquer first. A Wellness Program to Advance Girl Power, Health and Leadership, agrees. " It's important to help non-athletic girls develop some physical capability and confidence when they 're youthful. Whether it's through platoon or individual sports, girls need to form a physical relationship with their body that builds confidence.

Get girls working together. " Girls who work cooperatively in academia or who problem- break up do much better in taking large pitfalls or facing challenges. These girls report an inconceivable sense of accomplishment and feeling of capability, both of which give a huge boost to tone- regard,. Encourage your son to share in platoon- structure conditioning or join associations that calculate cooperation.

Let your son know you love her because of who she is, not because of what she weighs or how she looks. " Encourage your girl to eat in healthy ways, but don't over-obsess over what she eats. hear her opinions( about food, and other effects) and show appreciation for her oneness, to help her develop herself into the person she wants to be.

Comment on the way she carries herself into a room or the ideas she's expressing before opening on her aesthetics . She needs you to know her inwards and validate the developing person within, as well as noticing her arising youthful womanishness

Allow her to differ with you and get angry. Raising an important girl means living with one.

www.ingramcontent.com/pod-product-compliance
Lightning Source LLC
LaVergne TN
LVHW052115160826
845678LV00015B/3568